Fort Pitt Museum

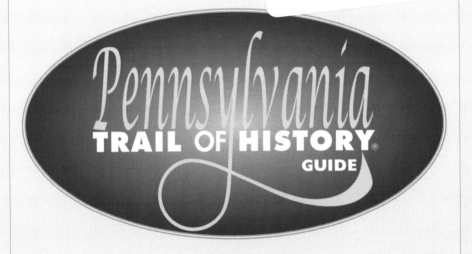

Text by David Dixon

STACKPOLE BOOKS

PENNSYLVANIA HISTORICAL
AND MUSEUM COMMISSION

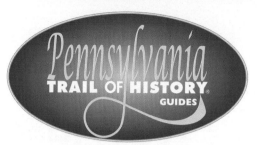

Kyle R. Weaver, Series Editor
Tracy Patterson, Designer

Published by
STACKPOLE BOOKS
5067 Ritter Road
Mechanicsburg, Pennsylvania 17055

Pennsylvania Trail of History® is a registered trademark of the Pennsylvania Historical and Museum Commission.

Printed in the United States of America
2 4 6 8 10 9 7 5 3 1
FIRST EDITION

Maps by Caroline Stover

Cover: Detail of *In the Shadow of the King* by Robert Griffing
PARAMOUNT PRESS
Page 3: Detail of pistol belonging to Gen. William Irvine
DON GILES/THE STATE MUSEUM OF PENNSYLVANIA
Page 5: Point State Park in Pittsburgh, site of Fort Pitt Museum
COMMONWEALTH MEDIA SERVICES

All other credits are noted throughout

Library of Congress Cataloging-in-Publication Data

Dixon, David.
    Fort Pitt Museum : Pennsylvania trail of history guide / text by David Dixon.
        p. cm.—(Pennsylvania trail of history guides)
    Includes bibliographical references.
    ISBN 0-8117-2972-9 (pbk.)
        1. Fort Pitt Museum—Guidebooks. 2. Point State Park (Pittsburgh, Pa.)—Guidebooks. 3. Fort Pitt (Pa.)—History. 4. Fort Duquesne (Pa.)—History. 5. Pittsburgh (Pa.)—French and Indian War, 1755–1763. 6. Frontier and pioneer life—Pennsylvania—Pittsburgh Region. 7. Pittsburgh Region (Pa.)—History—18th century. I. Title. II. Series.

F159.P68 F653 2004
940.2'534—dc22

                                                                                    2003024519

Contents

Editor's Preface

The city of Pittsburgh rose from the ashes of the continental dispute between Britain and France in the eighteenth century over control of the triangular landform at the Forks of the Ohio, a location considered the strategic key to dominating North America. Today, Fort Pitt Museum tells the story of this monumental rivalry with period artifacts and dramatic exhibits. Stackpole Books is pleased to continue its collaboration with the Pennsylvania Historical and Museum Commission (PHMC) to showcase the museum in this new volume of the Pennsylvania Trail of History Guides.

Each book in the series focuses on one of the historic sites or museums administered by the PHMC. The series was conceived and created by Stackpole Books with the cooperation of the PHMC's Division of Publications and Bureau of Historic Sites and Museums. Donna Williams heads the latter, and she and her staff of professionals review the text of each guidebook for accuracy and have made many valuable recommendations. Diane Reed, Chief of Publications, has facilitated relations between the PHMC and Stackpole from the project's inception, organized the review process with the commission, and attended to numerous details related to the venture. The first people at the commission I spoke to in 1998, when I originally developed the idea for a series of Trail of History guidebooks, were site administrators Michael Ripton, formerly of Ephrata Cloister; Douglas A. Miller, of Pennsbury Manor; and James A. Lewars, of Daniel Boone Homestead. The guidance and encouragement these gentlemen offered me led to discussions with the PHMC and the launching of the project.

For this volume, Chuck Smith, Administrator of Fort Pitt Museum, met with me in the early stages of the project to devise a workable outline. Douglas MacGregor, Museum Educator, provided expert guidance on finding available historic images to illustrate the guidebook. At Stackpole, David Reisch capably assisted me on production.

David Dixon, the author of the text, has a Ph.D. in American history from Kent State University and is professor of history at Slippery Rock University. He is the author of *Never Come to Peace Again: The Pontiac Indian Uprising of 1763–1765* and has already contributed to this series with the text for *Bushy Run Battlefield*. In this guidebook, he recounts the story of Fort Pitt and its role in the series of continental conflicts between the world powers of the eighteenth century, and follows with a brief tour of the Fort Pitt Museum and the park that was once the site of the most coveted land in North America.

Kyle R. Weaver, Editor
Stackpole Books

Introduction to the Site

Situated in the re-created Monongahela Bastion at Point State Park, the Fort Pitt Museum commemorates the strategic importance of the Forks of the Ohio during the Great War for Empire in which British, French, Colonial, and Native American forces struggled for control of North America. Through exhibits and programs, the museum also addresses the important role of Fort Pitt during the American Revolution and the early development of the city of Pittsburgh. The site presents tours, exhibits, educational programs, and publications to broaden understanding of the significance of the area known as "the Point." In meeting this goal, Fort Pitt Museum closely examines the French and Indian War, the American Revolution, the various military fortifications established on the site, the many cultures that influenced the development of the region, and the importance of the fur trade and other early commerce.

Fort Pitt Museum, one of twenty-six historic sites administered by the Pennsylvania Historical and Museum Commission, contains more than 12,000 square feet of exhibit space, an auditorium, galleries, and a gift shop. Also on the grounds of Point State Park, visitors can tour the Blockhouse, a structure that was once part of the fortifications and is presently owned and operated by the Daughters of the American Revolution; the outline of the fort's Music Bastion; the Flag Bastion overlooking the Monongahela River; and the outline of Fort Duquesne, a French outpost that preceded Fort Pitt. The museum staff is assisted by the Fort Pitt Museum Associates, a volunteer support group.

Outpost in the Wilderness

S tanding amidst the charred ruins of Fort Duquesne, Gen. John Forbes and his soldiers shivered in the cold November air. The temperature at the confluence of the Allegheny, Monongahela, and Ohio Rivers had dipped to a bone-chilling 16 degrees F, and many of the British troops were without adequate shelter, clothing, or shoes. Nonetheless, as the Union Jack fluttered above the burned ramparts on that frosty day in November 1758, it must have been a satisfying moment for Forbes and his men. For more than four years, the French had held control of the strategic Forks of the Ohio, using it as a base of operations to launch attacks against Colonial settlements east of the Appalachian Mountains. At last the British empire had gained its foothold west of the mountains, and an entire continent, ripe for conquest, lay beyond.

THE LAND, THE RIVERS, AND THE INDIANS

British occupation of the upper Ohio River Valley in 1758 marked but one phase in a long struggle for control over a region that offered so much to so many different people. The land beyond the Appalachian Mountains of Pennsylvania abounded in natural resources. Early European explorers were awed by the seemingly endless forests of oak, chestnut, hickory, ash, walnut, locust, and maple that covered the rolling landscape.

The rich forests served as the habitat for countless animals and birds, including deer, elk, bears, wildcats, wolves, turkey, and bison. Not only was the region rich in game, but it also supported numerous fur-bearing animals such as beavers, raccoons, and foxes, with whose pelts the Indians engaged in a lively trade with Europeans. Additionally, the many rivers and streams that coursed through the area teemed with fish. Missionary David Zeisberger noted the abundance of pike, buffalo fish, catfish, perch, and sturgeon. The waterways not only were a source of food, but also served as highways for trade and commerce. Zeisberger wrote of the region: "It is well watered by rivers and lakes so that it is possible to get almost anywhere by water. In the matter of trade, this is of great importance."

Col. George Washington of the Virginia Provincials. Promoted to lieutenant colonel of the Virginia militia in 1754 and to colonel a year later, Washington donned his uniform for Charles Willson Peale in 1772. It is the earliest known portrait of Washington. WASHINGTON-CUSTIS-LEE COLLECTION, WASHINGTON AND LEE UNIVERSITY, LEXINGTON, VIRGINIA

The area also was blessed with an abundance of mineral resources such as coal, petroleum, and limestone—all commodities that would one day fuel America's great age of industry. With such a wealth of resources, it is little wonder that the upper Ohio River Valley was coveted and used for thousands of years as a homeland by various native groups and attracted the attention of Europeans bent upon exploitation and settlement.

The powerful Iroquois Confederacy from New York invaded the area in the seventeenth century, displacing the original native occupants. In an effort to eliminate trade competitors and replenish bloodlines devastated by European diseases, the New York Iroquois dispersed the tribes of the upper Ohio in what has been called the Beaver Wars. The region became a veritable no-man's-land, occupied only by small bands of Iroquois hunters who were collectively referred to as Mingoes. Later, as European colonization along the Atlantic seaboard pressured other tribes, the Iroquois acquiesced to the relocation of these Indians into the Ohio Country. First came the Delawares who had once lived in the fertile Delaware River Valley. Either by their own volition or force, these people had gradually given up their land to agents operating on behalf of William Penn and his heirs. Some Delawares vacated their eastern homeland to settle along the Susquehanna, while others migrated westward across the mountains to build new communities along the Allegheny and Ohio Rivers. Soon they were joined by other small bands of refugees, such as the Shawnees, Mahicans, and Tuscaroras. Kin-based networking also helped attract Indians into the land beyond the mountains, as Mohawks, Oneidas, Onondagas, Cayugas, and Senecas joined their Mingo relatives.

The presence of so many different nations in the Ohio Country led to an expanding trade network that from time to time brought Hurons, Ottawas, Miamis, and other tribes to the banks of the Allegheny, Monongahela, and Ohio Rivers. Although these people represented various cultures and spoke many different languages, they quickly learned to coexist and formed multicultural communities in the Ohio Country. Despite their differences, they all came to recognize the region as a sanctuary from the increasing pressure of European encroachment. When Pennsylvania's Indian agent, Conrad Weiser, visited the village of Logstown (located along the Ohio River at present-day Ambridge) in 1748, he counted a total of 789 warriors representing the Seneca, Shawnee, Cayuga, Oneida, Mohawk, Huron, Mahican, and Delaware tribes. In council with these many nations, Weiser noted that they identified themselves as "all one People."

EMPIRES COLLIDE IN THE OHIO COUNTRY

As native people forged new homes and identities in the upper Ohio River Valley, two great European powers, Great Britain and France, also began to cast a covetous eye upon the territory. British interest in the Ohio Country was aroused when fur traders, financed by Philadelphia merchants, crossed over the mountains to purchase pelts from the Indians. Perhaps the most successful of these traders was George Croghan, an Irishman who emigrated to America in 1741. Within three short years, he was operating a trading post near the Forks of the Ohio. This operation consisted of a storehouse, several log houses, flat-bottomed barges and canoes, and ten acres planted in corn. From his base of operations near the confluence, Croghan branched out to establish other trading posts as far west as Sandusky, along the southern shore of Lake Erie.

At Quebec, French Colonial officials were alarmed over the incursion of the British into territory they claimed as part of the province of New France. The French were not only concerned about the competition in the fur trade, but also distressed by the fact that British penetration into the upper Ohio River Valley would sever ties between their possessions in Canada and the Mississippi River Valley. To counter this threat, the Canadian governor, the Marquis de La Galissonière, dispatched Capt. Pierre-Joseph Céloron de Blainville on an expedition with 230 soldiers to reassert authority over the Ohio Country and awe the Indian inhabitants into submitting to French hegemony. Céloron's command covered more than three thousand miles, stopping at the confluences of important watercourses to bury lead plates that proclaimed the territorial sovereignty of King Louis XV throughout the region. The Captain also held councils with numerous Indian leaders, in which he threatened, cajoled, and begged them to return to the French fold. The various tribal leaders were polite yet evasive. They asked the French officer who would supply them with necessary goods if the British were driven away.

When he returned to Montreal, Céloron reported on the situation among the Ohio Indians: "All I can say is that the nations of these localities are badly disposed toward the French, and are entirely devoted to the English. I do not know by what means they can be reclaimed." He concluded his report by suggesting that the French make "a strong defence" of the territory.

While George Croghan and other fur traders were conducting a brisk business on the frontier, other forces were at work in the British colonies to develop an

Chief of the Lenni Lenapes. *Once Europeans began to encroach on their Atlantic-seaboard homes in the seventeenth and eighteenth centuries, Indian tribes, including the Lenape (or Delaware), migrated west and resettled in places like the Ohio River Valley.*
THE LIBRARY COMPANY OF PHILADELPHIA

empire in the Ohio Country. A small group of Virginia aristocrats, including Thomas Lee, George Fairfax, Lawrence Washington (George's half-brother), and Virginia lieutenant governor Robert Dinwiddie, formed a partnership called the Ohio Company and applied to Great Britain's King George II for a 200,000 acre land grant around the Forks of the Ohio. These land speculators felt justified in their petition to the Crown, claiming that much of the upper Ohio River Valley was situated within the boundaries of Virginia according to its original charter. In July 1749, the king approved the Ohio Company's grant on the condition that one hundred families be settled on the land and a fort built in the region to protect them.

In the meantime, Pennsylvania governor James Hamilton protested what he called "the Stock and Scheme of the Virginia Company" and sent Lewis Evans to the Ohio Country to prepare a map that would prove that the land in question belonged to Pennsylvania. Evans finished his map in 1751, and Hamilton dashed off a letter to the British Lords of Trade insisting that his colony's boundaries extended as far west as Lake Erie and as far south as at least Logstown on the Ohio.

While Pennsylvania and Virginia squabbled over who owned the upper Ohio River Valley, the French acted to bolster their claims with military force. In the spring of 1753, the chevalier François le Mercier and seventy soldiers arrived at Presque Isle, a natural harbor along Lake Erie's southern shore. He had been directed by the new governor, Ange de Menneville, Marquis de Duquesne, to build a fort to secure New France's water route to the Ohio. Le Mercier's com-

pound was a rather simple structure of hewn logs stacked horizontally, with bastions at each corner and encompassing an area of about 120 square feet. In early June, le Mercier was reinforced by nearly eighteen hundred French soldiers and Canadian militia under the command of Capt. Pierre-Paul de la Malgue, Sieur de Marin.

The next step in Governor Duquesne's plan involved constructing a portage road to the headwaters of what later became known as French Creek. From this point, the French could float their canoes and bateaux, flat-bottomed, lightweight barges, downstream to the Allegheny, and from there to the Ohio. Marin and his men worked feverishly throughout the summer building their road to French Creek, where they erected another defensive outpost, Fort Le Boeuf. Further advance down the upper Ohio River Valley that summer was halted when Marin discovered that the waters of French Creek were too low to support his bateaux. He sent a small party of soldiers, under the command of Capt. Philippe-Thomas Chabert de Joncaire, to hold the confluence of French Creek and the Allegheny River at the Indian village of Venango (present-day Franklin). When Joncaire arrived at the village, he hoisted the French flag over a trading post once occupied by John Fraser, a Virginia blacksmith and fur trader who had been living among the Indians for more than a decade. Fraser had fled down the Allegheny in advance of Joncaire's occupation to spread the word to other British traders at Logstown. From there, news of the French invasion reached Philadelphia and Williamsburg, Virginia. The Pennsylvania Assembly, controlled by pacifist Quakers, failed to respond to the French threat. The Virginians, however, decided to take action.

The British and French in North America. *As their settlements spread beyond the Appalachians, the British came into conflict with the French, who had established forts and trading posts on the Ohio River and the Great Lakes. This imperial rivalry sparked the French and Indian War in 1754.*

CONFLICT IN THE OHIO COUNTRY

When Virginia lieutenant governor Dinwiddie learned of the French occupation of the Ohio Country, he quickly sent a dispatch to London asking for instructions from the home government. In October 1753, the governor received a reply directly from King George stating that he should send a diplomatic note to the French ordering them "peaceably to depart." Should the invaders fail to heed this demand, Dinwiddie was directed to "drive them off by force of arms."

To carry his letter to the French, the lieutenant governor selected twenty-one-year-old George Washington, a newly appointed major in the Virginia militia. What the young officer lacked in military knowledge, he made up for with boundless enthusiasm. With a small entourage of interpreters, Indian traders, and packers, Washington and his guide, Christopher Gist, set out from Wills Creek (present-day Cumberland, Maryland) on November 15. Within a week, the party had advanced as far as the strategic confluence at the Forks of the Ohio. It did not take a great deal of military experience for Washington to recognize that the vital point was "extremely well suited for a fort; as it has absolute command of both rivers." The young Virginian went on to observe that "the land at the point is twenty, or twenty-five feet above the common surface of the water; and a considerable bottom of flat, well timbered land all around it very convenient for building."

Washington continued northward with his men, arriving at Fort Le Boeuf on December 10. Here he tendered his diplomatic note to the new French commander, Legardeur de Saint-Pierre. Dinwiddie's message to the French was short and to the point. Claiming that the "lands upon the River Ohio, in the western parts of the Colony of Virginia, are so notoriously known to be the property of the Crown of Great Britain," the governor ordered the French to depart at once. Saint-Pierre's reply to Dinwiddie was equally terse: "As to the summons you send me to retire, I do not think myself obliged to obey it."

With the French response in hand, Washington hastened back to Virginia. When he arrived at Venango, the imprudent young major decided to leave his weak horses and tired companions behind and strike out on foot with Christopher Gist. Along the way, Washington was nearly shot by an Indian allied with the French and almost drowned in the icy waters of the Allegheny River. As he neared the settlement at Wills Creek, the major encountered a convoy of horses loaded with supplies under the direction of William Trent, now working for the Ohio Company. Trent's mission was to establish a company storehouse where Redstone Creek empties into the Monongahela River. From there, he intended to continue downriver and construct another company warehouse at the Forks of the Ohio.

Washington arrived at Williamsburg on January 16, 1754, and delivered his dispatches to Dinwiddie. The French refusal to abandon the Ohio Country allowed the lieutenant governor to take decisive military action. He gave William Trent a commission as a captain in the Virginia militia and ordered him to recruit a company of one hundred men. The governor also directed Trent to transform the proposed Ohio Company storehouse at the confluence of the three rivers into a military outpost that was to be called Fort Prince George. Captain Trent arrived at the Forks on February 17 and set about the task of laying out the fort. Tanacharison, a Seneca chief whom the English called the Half-King, came to the Point with a handful of warriors. The Half-King also was disconcerted over the

Washington's Expedition to Fort Le Boeuf.
In late fall 1753, the lieutenant governor of
Virginia dispatched George Washington to
the French fort near Lake Erie. Upon return-
ing in January 1754, the young major—and
former surveyor—sketched this map of his
journey. PENNSYLVANIA STATE ARCHIVES

French occupation of the Ohio Country
and encouraged Trent to hasten the construction of the outpost. In what was perhaps an ironic twist, it was Tanacharison
who personally laid the fort's first log.

Work progressed slowly for Trent and
his thirty-three men. With deep snow
blocking the mountain passes, obtaining
provisions from the settlement at Wills
Creek proved difficult. Finally, Captain
Trent left Ens. Edward Ward in charge of
construction and hurried back to Maryland to obtain more supplies. On April
13, Ward received word from an Indian

trader that a large number of French soldiers were moving down the Allegheny
to attack his position. The ensign quickly
threw up a palisade of logs around the
compound and had just hung the gate
on what was dubbed "Trent's Fort" when
the French force arrived. In a brief parley,
the French commander, Capt. Claude-
Pierre Pécaudy, Sieur de Contrecoeur,
informed Ward that he was hopelessly
outnumbered and demanded the surrender of the fort. Facing as many as six
hundred enemy troops, Ward had little
recourse but to comply. The French were
magnanimous in their victory, allowing
the British to take all their personal possessions and depart in peace.

After Ward's withdrawal, the French
dismantled the flimsy stockade and set
about building their own outpost. The
stronghold was named Fort Duquesne,
in honor of the new governor, the Marquis de Duquesne. This fort was larger
and considerably stronger than the crude
structures at Presque Isle and Le Boeuf.
The square enclosed five buildings,
including the commandant's house,
officer quarters, guardhouse, quartermas-
ter's store, and barracks. Protruding from
each corner of the fort were defensive
bastions, designed to provide enfilading
fire toward an attacking column. Within
the bastions were other structures,
including a kitchen, powder magazine,
ovens, and a blacksmith's shop. The two
curtain walls facing the land side were
constructed of earth packed between two
horizontal log walls. These twelve-foot-
thick walls were designed to withstand
light artillery fire. The palisade walls that
faced the Allegheny and Monongahela
Rivers were constructed in the usual fashion, with logs placed upright in a trench.
For further protection on the land side,
the French built two triangular fortifications known as ravelins, which could be
used as a first line of defense in case of

an attack. To complete the stronghold, a series of ditches and pickets surrounded the entire fort. Later, additional barracks were constructed to house the troops that would be sent from Canada to defend the French position in the upper Ohio River Valley.

While Contrecoeur and his men worked to complete Fort Duquesne, the Virginians were mounting their own invasion of the Ohio Country. On April 2, 1754, George Washington, recently promoted to lieutenant colonel, departed Alexandria at the head of two companies of Virginia militia. Col. Washington carried orders from Dinwiddie authorizing him to occupy and defend the confluence of the Ohio. When the column reached Wills Creek, Maryland, Washington learned that the French had arrived at the Forks first and compelled the surrender of Ensign Ward's small garrison. Undaunted, the young militia commander continued north to a narrow clearing in the dense forest known as Great Meadows, located a short distance from present-day Uniontown. Here Washington decided to establish a base camp and await reinforcements before launching an offensive against the French position at Fort Duquesne.

On May 27, an Indian arrived at the camp bearing a message from the Seneca chief, Tanacharison. The Half-King, camped a short distance away with a small party of his warriors, had discovered the tracks of French soldiers lurking nearby. Washington quickly assembled forty men and set out at nightfall to make contact with the Indians. After traveling throughout the night, the Virginians reached Tanacharison's camp shortly after dawn on May 28. The Seneca leader agreed to lead Washington to the French bivouac, located at the base of a nearby cliff. Cautiously approaching the French position, Washington deployed his force around the unsuspecting enemy. One of the Frenchmen spotted the soldiers on the cliff above and sounded the alarm. At the same time, young Washington gave the command to open fire. In the brief skirmish that followed, ten French soldiers were killed, including their commander, Ens. Joseph Coulon de Jumonville. The Virginians captured another twenty-one prisoners. One French soldier managed to escape, making his way back to Fort Duquesne to spread the alarm. With his prisoners in tow, Washington departed the field of battle that became known as Jumonville Glen and returned to his base camp at Great Meadows. Concerning this brief skirmish in the forest, the British statesman Horace Walpole later wrote, "The volley fired by a young Virginian in the backwoods of America set the world on fire."

Back at the Great Meadows, Washington hastily threw up a small stockade that he dubbed his "fort of necessity" and impatiently awaited reinforcements. Two additional companies of Virginia provincials and a contingent of British independent troops from South Carolina eventually arrived to augment Washington's tiny command. But these reinforcements, which totaled more than two hundred men, were not enough to stave off a French counterattack. On July 3, 1754, a mixed force of some seven hundred French and Indians surrounded Fort Necessity and opened fire. In what Washington later described as an "unequal fight, with an enemy sheltered behind the trees," the British and Virginian forces suffered terribly. By the end of the day, more than one hundred of his soldiers had been killed or wounded. Believing that more British reinforcements were on their way, the French commander, Capt. Louis Coulon de Villiers (Ensign Jumonville's half-brother), offered Washington an opportunity to surrender and peacefully

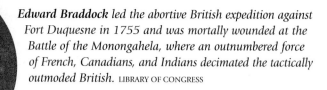

Edward Braddock led the abortive British expedition against Fort Duquesne in 1755 and was mortally wounded at the Battle of the Monongahela, where an outnumbered force of French, Canadians, and Indians decimated the tactically outmoded British. LIBRARY OF CONGRESS

depart. The following day, a dejected and humiliated Washington led his tattered command from the Great Meadows, leaving the entire upper Ohio River Valley in French control.

BRADDOCK'S DEFEAT

Following the surrender of Fort Necessity, it became apparent to British officials in London that the disjointed provinces in America were no match for France's monolithic Colonial empire. Accordingly, in March 1755, large numbers of British soldiers began to arrive in America. Two full regiments from Ireland—the 44th Regiment of Foot, under the command of Sir Peter Halket, and Col. Thomas Dunbar's 48th Regiment—disembarked at Alexandria, Virginia, to join provincial forces from Virginia, Maryland, and South Carolina for a thrust against Fort Duquesne. Overall command of the expedition fell to sixty-year-old Maj. Gen. Edward Braddock, a veteran of the elite Coldstream Guards. Although Braddock was a career soldier, much of his military experience had been gained in noncombat, supportive roles.

Rough terrain, a lack of provincial troops and wagons, the reluctance of the colonies to financially support the endeavor, and numerous other logistical problems hampered Braddock's campaign from the beginning. At virtually every turn, the general was frustrated by what he considered indifference on the part of the colonists he was sent to defend. Contractors failed to deliver promised provisions to feed the army

and the general was plagued by a lack of wagons to haul supplies. Additionally, though the governors of Virginia and Pennsylvania had assured Braddock that they would deliver an ample number of Indian allies to guide the command, in all but a few cases the warriors either did not show up or returned home in disgust due to the general's "pride and ignorance." The Oneida chief Monacatootha bitterly complained afterward that Braddock "looked upon us as dogs, and would never hear anything what was said to him . . . that was the reason that a great many warriors left him and would not be under his command."

After a month of delays, the expedition finally cleared Fort Cumberland at Wills Creek, Maryland, on June 9 and headed toward its greatest challenge: crossing the rugged Allegheny Mountains. The command numbered twenty-two hundred men, including two hundred axmen to cut a swath through the dense forest and fifty sailors whose experience at rigging proved useful in pulling the wagons and artillery over the mountains. Progress was slow, however, and it took the column ten days to advance a mere twenty-six miles. Fearing that the French would be able to reinforce Fort Duquesne before his arrival, Braddock called his officers together in a council of war. George Washington, who served as a volunteer aide, recommended that the general leave behind his cumbersome baggage train and advance as rapidly as possible toward the Forks of the Ohio with a "flying column" of soldiers. Braddock concurred with the young Virginian's advice and divided his command, selecting a mixed force of more than fourteen hundred regulars and provincials to move in rapid marches toward the enemy. Col. Thomas Dunbar, with most of the wagons, would follow "by slow and regular marches."

While General Braddock's army trudged through the forest, the French at Fort Duquesne prepared as best they could for the eventual assault. Captain Contrecoeur, the fort's commander, recognized that his wooden stockade could never withstand a bombardment by Braddock's heavy artillery. He was also skeptical that his small command, numbering less than six hundred French marine and Canadian militia, could defeat the British in open combat. Nonetheless, Contrecoeur had one notable advantage—a strong contingent of over eight hundred Indian allies. Most of these Ottawa, Potawatomie, Chippewa, and Huron warriors had entered the Ohio River Valley with the French invasion two years earlier. Also, a small group of Ohio Country Indians, mainly Shawnees and a few Delawares, had joined with the French following the expulsion of the British the year before.

With the British less than three days' march from the Forks, a frustrated Contrecoeur seemed poised to blow up the fort and retreat. At this point Capt. Daniel-Hyacinthe-Marie Liénard de Beaujeu, recently arrived from Canada, persuaded Contrecoeur to allow him to sortie out with a detachment of soldiers and most of the Indians in an attempt to ambush Braddock.

On July 9, Braddock's command crossed the Monongahela River unopposed. Surely, if the enemy were going to attack, this would have been the perfect opportunity. The British were now only ten short miles from their coveted objective, and the officers and men were jubilant over their good fortune. Once the column had re-formed, Braddock directed the vanguard, under the command of Col. Thomas Gage, to proceed down the trail toward the French stronghold. In their euphoria, the British failed to secure a hill that extend along their right flank. This would prove to be a costly mistake.

Rushing through the forest, Captain Beaujeu hoped to reach the river before the redcoats had crossed. With him was a meager force of 112 French soldiers, 146 Canadian militia, and 637 Indians. Without warning, the French and their Indian allies ran headlong into Colonel Gage's vanguard. Reacting quickly to the situation, Captain Beaujeu, who was dressed in Indian garb, signaled his native warriors to disperse along either side of the trail. At that moment, the front rank of Gage's column unleashed a deadly volley, instantly killing Beaujeu. The Indians, however, no longer needed this inspirational leader as they darted from tree to tree along the flanks of the British column. They quickly took up position along the hill and began to pour a deadly fire into Gage's right flank. The French regulars and militia held the front, while other warriors stealthily moved along the left side of the redcoat column. Fearing complete encirclement, Gage ordered a retreat.

Back with the main column, General Braddock heard the first rattle of musketry and rushed forward with the main column to reinforce the vanguard. The remnants of Gage's retreating men collided with the reinforcements rushing forward, creating confusion in the ranks. Perhaps as a result of prior direction, the Indians especially targeted the mounted British officers. This added to the panic, since disciplined British troops were reluctant to act without orders from their officers. As a result, the redcoats huddled together in the open road, firing wildly into the woods at an enemy they could not see. In some cases, the frightened troops massed in the roadway fired at their own men.

Riding forward, General Braddock tried in vain to restore order, cursing and lashing out at the panic-stricken soldiers with the flat side of his sword. Washington rode up and pleaded with Braddock to allow him to scatter three hundred men throughout the trees and fight Indian fashion. The general lifted his saber and angrily replied: "I've a mind to run you through the body. We'll sup today in Fort Duquesne or else in hell!"

After three hours of fighting, the redcoats began to run low on ammunition. Many of them had expended their full complement of twenty-four cartridges and had never seen an enemy. First in small bunches, and then en masse, the British threw down their weapons and fled the battlefield. Braddock fought on, frantically trying to rally his men until a musket ball penetrated his side and lodged in a lung. The general tumbled from the saddle and was carried off the field in a litter made from his own sash. A group of officers loaded the commander into a cart as the remnants of his army, seized by horror and confusion, fled in wild panic.

The Battle of the Monongahela was over. Out of a total force of more than fourteen hundred men, nearly nine hundred had been killed or wounded, including sixty-three of Braddock's eighty-six officers. In addition, the British lost all of their artillery, seventeen barrels of gunpowder, more than four hundred horses, one hundred head of cattle, nearly two thousand musket cartridges, and the payroll chest containing £25,000 in currency. In comparison, the French and Indians suffered less than fifty casualties.

The wounded General Braddock lingered in agony for nearly five days, as the stunned British force made its long retreat back to Colonel Dunbar's camp. Even while he lay dying, the old soldier could not believe what had happened. "Who would have thought it," he was heard to mutter. Before he died, Braddock delivered one statement that proved to be prophetic: "We shall know better how to deal with them another time." After the general's death, Dunbar chose to continue the retreat, once again leaving the Ohio Country in undisputed control of the French.

Braddock's disastrous defeat persuaded many of the Ohio Country Indians to finally ally themselves with the French. They could use their association with the forces of Louis XV to regain land lost to the British east of the mountains; to assert their independence from the nominal control of the Iroquois to the north; and to obtain valuable trade goods.

The French commanders at Fort Duquesne inspired the Indians to launch deadly raids into the backcountry settlements. As a result of these attacks, hundreds of backcountry inhabitants fled their homes to find sanctuary in more settled areas to the east. By July 1756, the new commandant of Fort Duquesne, Capt. Jean-Daniel Dumas, could boast that he had "succeeded in ruining the three adjacent provinces, Pennsylvania, Maryland, and Virginia, driving off the inhabitants, and totally destroying the settlements over a tract of country thirty leagues wide."

Despite the havoc created by these Indian raids, the British government offered no relief for the distressed frontier settlers. It might have been expected that following Braddock's defeat, the home government in London would have reconcentrated its efforts to seize the Forks of the Ohio and repel the French. The affairs of the American colonies, however, assumed a role of secondary importance when Great Britain officially declared war on France in May 1756. Military officials in London became more concerned with fighting the French on the continent of Europe and virtually left the colonists to fend for themselves. The Pennsylvania Assembly, dominated by pacifist Quakers and determined to safeguard their power to control appropriations, fervently debated the defense issue. A number of Quakers resigned from the Assembly rather than compromise their principles. In the end, with Indian war parties overrunning the frontier, there was little recourse but to adopt measures that called for the construction of a chain of forts along Blue Mountain and the recruitment of two battalions of provincial troops to provide for the colony's defense. More insidious was the offer made by Gov. Robert Hunter Morris to pay a bounty for Indian scalps.

One of the battalion commanders, Col. John Armstrong, insisted that defense measures alone could not stop the Indian raids. As a result, he proposed that the Pennsylvanians launch a punitive strike against one of the principal Indian staging areas—the Delaware village of Kittanning, located along the Allegheny River north of Fort Duquesne. The village was the supposed stronghold of the noted war leader, Captain Jacobs, whose warriors had terrorized the frontier.

Setting out from Fort Shirley (present-day Shirleysburg) with three hundred men, Colonel Armstrong reached the village at dawn on September 8, 1756. The Indians, who thought themselves secure, being so far removed from

44th Regiment of Foot. *When the British government realized that colonial militias could not fend off the French, soldiers of this Irish regiment were among the first to be sent to the colonies.* THE ROYAL COLLECTION © 2004, HER MAJESTY QUEEN ELIZABETH II

the British settlements, were completely surprised when the provincials rushed into their town. Many of the warriors fled to Captain Jacobs's house, where they put up a stiff resistance, firing at the soldiers outside. Finally one of the Pennsylvanians set fire to the structure. Some of the Indians burned to death inside, while others came tumbling out only to be shot down by the soldiers. The provincials then set fire to the entire town and pulled back to a nearby hilltop. Gunpowder stored inside many of the bark covered dwellings exploded.

In the Kittanning raid, Armstrong lost nearly forty men in dead and wounded. For the Indians, the attack was far more devastating—Captain Jacobs, his wife, and perhaps as many as thirty other Delawares were killed. Their town and all of its provisions were lost. Per-haps most significantly, the Indians no longer felt secure in their homeland. The Delawares informed Capt. Jean-Daniel Dumas, the commander of Fort Duquesne, that "they would no longer continue in any Place between them [the French] and the English, but would remove to the other side of Fort Duquesne, as a Place of greater Safety."

THE FORBES CAMPAIGN

While the raid against Kittanning may have been an important psychological victory for the Pennsylvanians, it did little to quell Indian attacks on the frontier. Throughout 1757, Ohio Country warriors continued to raid settlements in the Juniata and Susquehanna River Valleys. The British fared no better with military affairs in Europe. In July 1757, an allied army led by the Duke of Cumberland suffered a crushing defeat at the hands of a French army at the Battle of Hastenbeck in Hanover. After the battle, Cumberland agreed to disband his army, leaving Britain's sole ally, Prussia, to fight alone on the continent of Europe. The resulting political and military chaos led to the ascendancy of William Pitt as secretary of state. Pitt, along with his chief military advisor, Sir John Ligonier, immediately set about to devise a new strategy to defeat France. He reasoned that the best way to contend with French military power was to use Great Britain's naval superiority to its greatest extent. British ships could blockade ports and transport troops to seize French colonies. The Royal Navy could also be called upon to harass French commercial shipping.

Pitt and his advisors also believed that greater emphasis should be placed on the war in America. As a result, the secretary developed a plan for 1758 that called for a three-pronged offensive against New France. The first phase of

An Iroquois Warrior. Indians made up well over half the French force that attacked Braddock's army. Native tactics and European weaponry were a deadly combination.
NATIONAL ARCHIVES OF CANADA

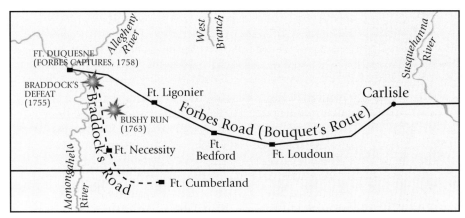

Braddock's Expedition. *General Braddock led his force west out of Fort Cumberland and north toward Fort Duquesne in June 1755. He met defeat at the Monongahela a month later.*

the operation called for British forces under Gen. Jeffery Amherst to seize the French fortress at Louisbourg on Cape Breton Island. This citadel helped guard the entrance into the St. Lawrence River. If Louisbourg fell, it would be far more difficult for the French to supply Canada. The second prong would be led by Gen. James Abercromby, who would command an army to assault the French along the Lake George–Lake Champlain corridor. If the redcoats seized enemy strongholds at Ticonderoga and Crown Point, it would open this corridor to a British invasion of Montreal and the Canadian heartland. The third and final campaign in Pitt's strategy called for yet another expedition against Fort Duquesne. Once the Forks of the Ohio came under British control, the other French outposts to the north would fall like dominoes.

To lead the campaign, British policy makers chose Brig. Gen. John Forbes, a Scotsman known for his ambition and attention to military details. The fifty-year-old Forbes arrived in Philadelphia in mid-April and immediately began organizing his expedition. Forbes's plan involved a "protected advance" over the mountains that would lead to Fort

Duquesne. Unlike Braddock, the general decided to move his army across Pennsylvania in stages, pausing at regular intervals along the march to construct forts that could be used as supply depots and for defensive purposes should his army be overwhelmed. These forts could also serve to keep open the line of communication from the frontier to Philadelphia. To execute his plans, the general assembled a mixed force of regular and provincial soldiers, including the 60th Royal American Regiment and a detachment of the 77th Regiment of Foot, better known as Montgomery's Highlanders, recruited from Scotland to serve in the North American campaigns. The Colonial troops came from Pennsylvania, Virginia, Delaware, Maryland, and North Carolina.

Throughout the early spring and summer, Forbes remained behind in Philadelphia gathering supplies and arranging contracts for wagons and draft animals. He was gravely ill from an intestinal malady, perhaps colon cancer, and the day-to-day activities of the campaign were handled by his second-in-command, Col. Henry Bouquet. This Swiss soldier of fortune had come to America in 1756 to command the Royal

John Forbes. Chosen to lead another expedition against Fort Duquesne in 1758, the gravely ill General Forbes accompanied his army on a litter and took Fort Duquesne in November. He died a few months later. CARNEGIE LIBRARY OF PITTSBURGH

American Regiment, a unit recruited among the German-speaking colonists. Colonel Bouquet took the advance reaching Carlisle in mid-May. After accumulating sufficient supplies, wagons, horses, and men, he moved westward to the provincial outpost called Fort Loudoun.

Leaving Fort Loudoun, Bouquet moved northward, skirting the eastern slope of Tuscarora Mountain before crossing over the ridge at what became known as Cowen's Gap, and then proceeding west to another provincial outpost, Fort Lyttleton. From there, Bouquet and his force pushed on, reaching Raystown on June 24. The colonel's chief engineer, Capt. Harry Gordon, set about the task of transforming the tiny trading village into a fortified camp large enough to accommodate more than fifteen hundred troops. While Gordon's crew worked to complete the compound, named Fort Bedford, Bouquet trained his regular and provincial forces to fight a new kind of war. Having learned from Braddock's debacle at the Monongahela, the colonel developed new tactics that called for lead elements of an army on the march to "detach Small Parties a Mile forward, who Shall march in great Silence, and visit carefully all Suspected Places, as Copses, Ditches, and Hallows, where ambuscades may be concealed." Joseph Shippen, one of the officers with the Pennsylvania provincials, observed Bouquet drilling troops at Fort Bedford

and wrote, "Every afternoon he exercises his men in the woods and bushes in a particular manner of his own invention, which will be of great service in an engagement with the Indians."

By September, Bouquet's advance force had cleared the final hurdle of Laurel Ridge and established a camp at Loyalhanna Creek, called Fort Ligonier. From here, only fifty miles from the Forks of the Ohio, General Forbes hoped to mass his six-thousand-man army and make the final thrust against Fort Duquesne. Conditions at the French outpost had deteriorated significantly during the summer of 1758. The new commandant, Capt. François-Marie de Marchand, Sieur de Ligneris, found himself short on men, provisions, and Indian allies. From the very beginning, Colonial officials in Quebec had found it difficult to keep this wilderness outpost supplied. A great deal of the provisions coming into the fort came from the Illinois Country or faraway Louisiana. To compound the problem, the 1758 British offensive completely stopped the trickle of supplies coming from Canada. In August, a British force under the command of Col. John Bradstreet seized Fort Frontenac at the head of the St. Lawrence River. This citadel controlled the flow of all reinforcements and supplies to the Ohio Country from the north. De Ligneris had to be content with the troops at hand and his devoted Indian allies.

By late summer, however, the loyalty of the Indians surrounding Fort Duquesne was beginning to waver. While many of the Great Lakes warriors and Canadian Indians remained steadfast, the Ohio Country natives sensed a weakening of France's once firm grasp. Powder, lead, and provisions, which had once been plentiful, all but dried up. With so few men and supplies, the Indians questioned how De Ligneris would be able to fend off the huge redcoat army that inched forward toward the Ohio. General Forbes did all he could to reinforce Indian concern over the weakness of the French and the size of British forces. At the same time, the general wanted the Ohio Country Indians to know that the British had no desire to push them out and take their land. Working through the Quaker's Friendly Association, Forbes sent Christian Frederick Post as an emissary to the Delawares to reassure them that once the French had been turned out of the upper Ohio River Valley, the redcoats would likewise return east, back over the mountains. All the general asked was that the warriors stand aside in the impending conflict. Peace advocates, such as the Delaware chief Tamaqua, encouraged the Indians to listen to the British entreaties.

When Colonel Bouquet reached Fort Ligonier on September 7, scouts informed him that the French forces at Fort Duquesne were in a weakened condition. Maj. James Grant, an officer in the 77th Highland Regiment, proposed a reconnaissance in force against the enemy. Although Colonel Bouquet may have been reluctant to acquiesce to Grant's request before the rest of Forbes's army had arrived, he could still see the advantages to such an enterprise. While gathering valuable intelligence for the final thrust toward the enemy position, Grant's soldiers could also give the enemy a taste of their own medicine by launching a guerrilla-style sortie against the outlying French pickets and nearby Indian villages. Consequently, Bouquet gave his consent to the reconnaissance.

Bouquet instructed Grant to take a mixed force of eight hundred Highlanders and provincials, reconnoiter Fort Duquesne, attempt to destroy any Indian camps in the vicinity, and then retire his force in an enticing manner to draw any pursuers into an ambush posted along either side of the trail. This plan reveals that Bouquet had learned a great deal about the nature of frontier warfare. The colonel reasoned that the Indians, enraged over an attack on their villages, would view the retreating troops as a sign of impending victory and charge headlong into the ambush that awaited them along Grant's return route.

But Grant and his junior officers did not follow through on the proposed ruse. After setting fire to a few blockhouses that served as sentinel posts, Grant remained on a rise overlooking Fort Duquesne. Perceiving the enemy as too weak to sally out of their stronghold and fight him, the major sent one hundred Highlanders down the hill, straight toward the fort. The French and their Indian allies, perhaps as many as eight hundred in number, poured out of the compound and quickly encircled these Scottish soldiers. Grant and his reserve force rushed into the fray to rescue their beleaguered comrades and found themselves hemmed in on all sides. Hearing the firing coming from the direction of Fort Duquesne, the troops Grant had held in ambush along the trail also rushed forward and joined the fight. Confusion reigned as the major attempted to rally his men. It was like Braddock's defeat all over again. Eventually the redcoat force broke and retreated, leaving behind nearly three hundred casualties, including Major Grant, who was captured.

General Forbes, so gravely ill that he had to be transported in a litter slung

THE ROYAL AMERICAN REGIMENT

Many of the British soldiers who served at the remote frontier outposts, including Fort Pitt, came from the 60th Regiment of Foot, better known as the Royal American Regiment. By 1756, Great Britain faced a serious challenge in supplying troops to fight in America, due to both the low number of recruits in Britain and the high cost of transporting soldiers across the ocean. As a result, the king's cabinet decided to raise four battalions in America. Initially, the ministers hoped to fill the ranks from the Protestant German population in Pennsylvania. Foreign officers, such as Henry Bouquet, were offered commissions in the British Army to train and lead these troops. As it turned out, the 60th Regiment of Foot proved to be more cosmopolitan than expected. Less than eighteen percent of the men in the regiment came from the German communities in America, while another fifty-five percent came from English, Irish, or Scottish stock, and the remainder were recruited from a variety of foreign countries in Europe.

Considering the ethnic diversity of such a military unit, it is not surprising that cohesiveness was difficult to achieve at first. At one point, two of the regiment's officers fought a duel to the death when one of the men "damned all the Germans, saying they were a Parcell of Rascalls, and imposing Scoundrells." Despite any ethnic tension that may have existed in the unit, the soldiers achieved a high level of esprit de corps and an enviable reputation due to their impressive combat record.

In 1758, the Royal Americans led the vanguard of John Forbes's army as it struggled over the Allegheny Mountains. Other battalions of the regiment participated in the ill-fated expedition to seize Fort Ticonderoga and in the successful campaign against the fortress at Louisbourg. The following year, the men of the 60th took part in the siege of Quebec, scaling the steep cliff to engage the French on the Plains of Abraham. In 1760, the Royal American Regiment accompanied Gen. Jefery Amherst in his campaign against Montreal. These engagements provided the regiment with their motto *"Celer et Audax"*—"Swift and Bold."

When the fighting ended in the French and Indian War, two battalions of the regiment were disbanded, and the remaining soldiers dispersed to garrison the forts in the western frontier. The Royal Americans bore the brunt of Pontiac's Uprising as the Indians overran the small outposts located in the Great Lakes region and along the Venango Trail. At Detroit

between two horses, regarded Grant's defeat as a great disappointment. Nonetheless, he became even more determined to avenge the loss of so many soldiers by seizing the French fort at the confluence. These sentiments were shared by the men in the ranks. "The Troops now breathe nothing but revenge," wrote one provincial officer. Time was running out for Forbes's army, however, as winter was approaching the ridges of the Laurel Highlands. Forbes and the remainder of the army did not arrive at Fort Ligonier until early November, and the general was in a quandary regarding whether to launch an immediate assault upon the French or wait until spring. On November 11, Forbes held a council with his officers, most of whom favored postponing an attack against the French. The following day, the French made a weak sortie against Fort Ligonier. During the encounter, the redcoats managed to take several prisoners. One of them was a renegade named Johnson who, years before, had been captured by the Indians in the Lancaster Valley. Under interrogation, Johnson revealed that the garrison at Fort Duquesne amounted to less than five hundred men and that virtually all of

Along Laurel Ridge. *In this painting by John Buxton, members of the Royal American Regiment pause near Loyalhanna Creek, where General Forbes planned to assemble his army for the final fifty miles to Fort Duquesne, September 1758.* PARAMOUNT PRESS

and Fort Pitt, the beleaguered soldiers managed to withstand the Indian attacks during the long summer of 1763. A contingent of Royal Americans accompanied their commander, Col. Henry Bouquet, as he led a relief force to Fort Pitt. During the desperate fighting at Bushy Run, twelve members of the regiment were killed or wounded.

The 60th Regiment of Foot later participated in the American Revolution, but by this time, most of the rank and file were recruited in Great Britain and Hanover.

the Indian allies had deserted the French. With this valuable piece of intelligence, Forbes decided to continue his advance against the enemy.

Back at Fort Duquesne, Captain De Ligneris took stock of his situation. He had less than three hundred effective troops. Many of the Indians had returned home following Grant's defeat. The others, mostly Ohio Country tribes, had abandoned the French as a result of Christian Frederick Post's peace initiative, formalized by a treaty council held at Easton in late October. In addition, De Ligneris could not hope for aid from Canada due to the fall of Frontenac. The captain had no other recourse but to remove the artillery from the bastions, load his batteau with what meager supplies he had left, and set fire to the fort. Some of the French floated down the Ohio toward the Illinois Country, while others traveled north to winter at Venango.

On November 25, 1758, Forbes's main column marched into the coveted triangle. The next day, the general wrote a dispatch to his superiors informing them of his victory. He began his communication by stating that his letter came from "Fort Duquesne now Pittsbourg."

The Ends of the American Earth

Although the French had been driven from the Forks of the Ohio, John Forbes and Henry Bouquet still feared that their victory was in jeopardy. It was the dead of winter, and the British Army was more than three hundred miles from Philadelphia. It would be impossible to transport supplies over the mountains to sustain such a large force. The only recourse was to discharge many of the provincials and withdraw the army back over the mountains, leaving behind a skeleton garrison of two hundred men to occupy the hard-won triangle. On December 4, the general, carried in his litter, led the vanguard of his army on the back trail toward Philadelphia.

The general left behind a force of less than 250 provincial soldiers to hold the strategic point until supplies and reinforcements could be brought west in the spring. Bouquet gave command of the coveted triangle to Col. Hugh Mercer, a Scottish physician who had gained recognition as a natural leader. He had served as a captain in one of the Pennsylvania battalions and fought with Armstrong at the raid on Kittanning. By the time of the Forbes campaign, Mercer had become a seasoned veteran who could be relied upon to hold the strategic Forks of the Ohio during the dead of winter, even with the enemy still lurking to the north.

Mercer's immediate concerns involved building adequate shelter for the troops and keeping tabs on the disposition of the French. He set to work constructing a new military post around the ruins of Fort Duquesne and by mid-January was able to send Bouquet a satisfactory report on his progress. Although nothing had been completed at this time, Mercer had begun to build barracks, storehouses, and a stockade that enclosed everything. Mercer's Fort became the third outpost to occupy the Forks of the Ohio. Throughout the cold winter months of 1759, Mercer's position at Pittsburgh continued to improve. The entrenchments around the fort were completed, and the tiny garrison was reinforced by troops from the Royal American Regiment. A large quantity of Indian trade goods arrived to satisfy the growing conglomeration of Ohio natives camped around the fort.

The Struggle for North America. During the 1700s, the continent was the scene of several major wars, in which colonial soldiers with their backwoods tools of war—such as the powder horn shown here—encountered the modern military might of European powers. POINT STATE PARK

On March 11, 1759, General Forbes died in Philadelphia. Gen. Jeffrey Amherst, the overall British commander in North America, selected Brig. Gen. John Stanwix to replace Forbes and oversee the construction of a much stronger outpost at Pittsburgh. Even from his distant headquarters in New York, Amherst could see the strategic importance of the confluence. He told Bouquet that the point "is a Post of the greatest Consequence, great Care must be taken to Keep it in Respectable Condition, and all means must be used to protect & Defend it." Clearly, Amherst intended the new post at Pittsburgh to serve as the main staging point for a British offensive northward to seize and occupy all the French forts remaining in the Ohio Country and beyond to the Great Lakes.

Throughout the summer of 1759, Captain Mercer and the Indian agent, George Croghan, continued to assure the natives that the British had no designs upon their land. At one conference, Croghan told a large assembly of Ohio and Great Lakes tribes that once the French were finally driven away, "the General will depart your Country after securing our Trade with you and our Brethren to the Westward." Despite these promises, the Delaware, Shawnee, Mingo, and other tribes looked on with suspicion as the Royal engineer, Capt. Harry Gordon, arrived at the Forks of the Ohio in late summer with more than three hundred artificers to begin construction on Fort Pitt.

The new outpost at the confluence was a complex series of fortifications that covered seventeen acres. Instead of a crude stockade of wood, the curtain walls were built from earth, which was covered with sod laid like bricks perpendicular to the sloping walls to keep them from eroding. On the land side, these earthen works were supported by brick and masonry retaining walls. Inside the curtain walls were casements and magazines used to store supplies and ammunition. Five huge earth bastions projected from the walls of the fort. The points of these bastions were reinforced with limestone. Running along the inside of the walls were barracks, officers' quarters, a storehouse, and a two-story brick house for the commandant. The interior buildings surrounded a parade ground that encompassed more than an acre. A series of ditches, redoubts, and ravelins formed the outer works of Fort Pitt. For access to the inner works of the fort, two drawbridges were built across the ditches. Gordon and his construction crew worked for two years to complete the sprawling complex, only to have their efforts nearly destroyed by a devastating flood that caused considerable damage in January 1762. The following spring, another flood washed away the sod that covered one of the bastions and curtain walls.

LIFE AT FORT PITT

While the new fort at the triangle continued to grow, so did the civilian population outside the compound. The first to arrive at Pittsburgh were the fur traders, anxious to resume their lucrative commerce with the Indians. As early as February 1759, Lt. Caleb Graydon, a Pennsylvania provincial officer stationed at Fort Lyttleton, counted forty-five sutlers and Indian traders headed west with nearly 250 packhorses laden with goods for both soldiers and Indians. The following month, another forty-two enterprising souls carried merchandise such as rum, flour, molasses, shoes, and tobacco past the post. Surprisingly, one of these merchants was a woman, Catherine Winepilt, who guided a packhorse bearing apples and eggs to sell to the garrison and neighboring Indians. Before long, a substantial community of traders, merchants, tavernkeepers, speculators, and laborers sprang up outside the walls of Fort Pitt. Colonel Bouquet conducted a census in April 1761 and discovered that Pittsburgh contained a total of 160 structures, with a population of 219 men, 75 women, and 38 children. Most of these structures were log cabins, storehouses, grog shops, or ramshackle huts.

Bouquet regarded most of the settlement's inhabitants as a useless and indolent lot. The raw frontier community drew opportunists of every kind, and Bouquet complained that "This Place is Particularly infested with a number of Inhabitants the Scum of the neighboring Provinces, who have no visible means to live, except a License, & think it bad Consequence for the garrison, and I could wish the number of Traders was limited & obliged to give security for their Behaviour." One evening while Bouquet was at supper, thieves broke into his quarters within the walls of the fort and stole money intended for both his personal use and military subsistence. The incident prompted the colonel to label Pittsburgh "a Colony sprung from Hell for the Scourge of mankind."

Life at the remote frontier community of Pittsburgh proved for many to be a bitter disappointment. James Kenney, a Quaker trader from Philadelphia who arrived at the confluence early, provided a realistic picture of conditions at Fort Pitt. In a daily journal of activities at the Forks, Kenney's entries reveal that the environment was far from healthy, as inhabitants were constantly beset by diseases such as measles, smallpox, dysentery, and a deadly intestinal disorder described as the "flux." Sanitary conditions within the squalid dwellings left much to be desired, and Kenney complained of his trading post being infested with fleas that kept him awake at night. He also noted that the back-

country attracted a violent breed of men and the slightest insult could result in death. In September 1761, he recorded that a teamster had been brutally murdered for striking another man's dog.

While frontier settlers suffered innumerable hardships in the wilderness environment, it was likely worse for the soldiers who garrisoned Fort Pitt and the other far-flung outposts. With few exceptions, the common soldiers, both regular and provincial, were recruited from the lower classes and considered little more than pawns by the officers who commanded them. With their discipline and rigorous training, British regulars considered themselves superior to their Colonial counterparts. On the other hand, Colonial troops had little regard for such training and considered themselves well adapted for frontier combat. Despite these differences, both redcoats and provincials shared the misery that accompanied frontier military duty. Rations were often rancid, the pay was meager, barracks were foul and cramped, and punishment for even minor infractions was brutal. A soldier could receive a thousand lashes for stealing a keg of beer. The troops were commonly at the mercy of corrupt traders who cheated the men and kept them well supplied with alcohol. Colonel Bouquet finally issued orders forbidding his soldiers to enter Pittsburgh homes or taverns after dark. Like their civilian counterparts, soldiers were dissipated by alcohol and succumbed to the ravages of diseases such as smallpox. This dreaded scourge moved west with the army and plagued Fort Pitt for months. With all the hardships the troops were forced to endure, it is not surprising that desertion was commonplace at Fort Pitt and the other outposts along Forbes's Road.

Like the men in the ranks, officers also suffered from the privations of frontier duty. They frequently complained about a lack of supplies, forage for livestock, ammunition, rations, and even writing paper. Under such conditions, discipline and morale were difficult to maintain.

Within a few short years, the Forks of the Ohio bore little resemblance to the pristine wilderness that had once existed. The rapid despoilment of the land was an increasing concern to the Indians, who grew resentful over the pestilence that always seemed to accompany the white man's presence. Despite this growing uneasiness, a spirit of cross-cultural exchange and cooperation between the Europeans and Indians began to emerge on the trans-Appalachian frontier. Colonel Bouquet sent carpenters to the Delaware village of Tuscarawas, located along the Muskingum River, to build a house for Tamaqua. He also ordered the construction of a house and some stables for another Delaware leader known as Grey Eyes, who lived along the nearby Beaver River, and a two-story council house for the Indians near Fort Pitt. Surgeons at Fort Pitt provided medical care for the local Indian population, and the physicians also learned a great deal from the Indians, who pointed out the healing qualities of many herbal remedies. Delaware, Shawnee, and Mingo warriors introduced the British to other natural wonders. Sometimes the Indians brought the teeth and tusks of extinct woolly mammoths to Fort Pitt to show interested onlookers. They also served as guides for John Bartram, America's first botanist, and helped him collect specimens of vegetation unknown to the European world. Indians were, in fact, regularly employed as scouts, couriers, packhorse drivers, and laborers across the frontier. As a consequence, Indian people became familiar with European economics. The trader James Kenney,

who was accustomed to simply bartering merchandise for furs, began to record many cash transactions in his ledger.

PONTIAC'S UPRISING

Amid this cooperation and cross-cultural exchange, ominous signs of discontent emerged among the native people. Following the surrender of Montreal in 1760, the French presence in the trans-Appalachian frontier all but disappeared. With the French gone, Indians living in the Ohio Country and Great Lakes areas faced a series of policy changes introduced by the British military commander Jeffrey Amherst, due in part to Britain's need to economize following the end of fighting in North America. Elsewhere around the world, France and England were still at war, fighting in India, Africa, and the Caribbean. The war had been costly, plunging Great Britain into debt approaching £150 million, with 60 percent of the nation's budget going to pay the interest on that debt. Without question, precious resources had to be diverted from America to other theaters of operation in order to continue the struggle against France. As a result, Amherst was ordered to economize as much as possible.

Because of his contempt for the native people, the general viewed the Indian Department as the best place to cut spending. He eliminated the long-standing practice of providing Indian leaders with gifts that they regarded as a traditional part of the protocol that accompanied any negotiations. This was more than just a breach in diplomacy, indicating to the Indians that the British regarded them with contempt. Amherst also insisted that trade with the Indians be confined to military posts, thus forcing them to travel long distances in order to obtain valuable trade goods. Even more debilitating for the woodland warriors

In the Shadow of the King. *Indians ascend the rocky heights opposite Fort Pitt in this painting by Robert Griffing. Despite the fort and settlement that had risen out of the wilderness, Indians remained in the vicinity and sometimes cooperated with the British.* PARAMOUNT PRESS

was the fact that the general severely curtailed the sale of arms and ammunition. Most Indians had become almost wholly dependent upon firearms for hunting purposes, and limits on the sale of powder, lead, and muskets would mean starvation for many villages. Worst of all was the fact that despite their promises, the British refused to withdraw from Indian land. Instead, the redcoats now occupied all the former French forts and had built even bigger strongholds such as Fort Pitt.

Desperately seeking solutions to the challenges that they faced, many native people turned to prophecy and religion. One of the more influential prophets to emerge at this time was Neolin, a Delaware mystic who lived deep in the Ohio Country along the Tuscarawas River. He told his followers that "all ye Sins & Vices ye Indians have learned [came] from ye White people." In order to follow the "Good Road" to heaven, Neolin insisted that they must divest themselves of contact with the British and live in a more traditional fashion, "supporting themselves as their forefathers did." By doing so, he said, they would soon be able to drive the whites from their land.

Indian discontent finally exploded into violence in May 1763, when a confederation of Great Lakes tribes under the Ottawa leader Pontiac laid siege to Fort Detroit. Within weeks, Pontiac's warriors were able to destroy four smaller British forts in the vicinity. Inspired by the Ottawa chief's bold initiative, the Chippewas attacked Fort Michilimackinac at the straits between Lakes Huron and Michigan. The entire garrison of thirty-eight men was either killed or taken into captivity. Throughout the summer and fall, the Indians maintained

Fort Pitt under Siege. *As Pontiac's Uprising engulfed Fort Detroit, emboldened tribes launched attacks in the Ohio Country, eventually encircling Fort Pitt in late spring 1763, as depicted by Robert Griffing in this painting. Escalating their siege in July, the Indians left on August 1 to meet Bouquet's forces at Bushy Run.* PARAMOUNT PRESS

a tight cordon around Detroit, and it was with great difficulty that the garrison was finally relieved by troops crossing Lake Erie from Fort Niagara.

The Delawares, Shawnees, and Mingoes who lived in the Ohio Country were equally inspired by Pontiac's defiance. On May 28, a war party struck William Clapham's farmstead along the Youghiogheny River, only twenty-five miles from Pittsburgh. The next day, Indians attacked and killed two soldiers working at a sawmill near Fort Pitt. The commandant of the fort, Capt. Simeon Ecuyer, was hardly prepared to bear the brunt of an Indian war. He had only 145 men of the Royal American Regiment to defend the outpost, which had been severely damaged by spring floods. The flood water had also destroyed a considerable quantity of flour and other rations. Nonetheless, the determined Captain Ecuyer prepared as best he could for an all-out siege. He brought nearly

four hundred civilians inside the fort and ordered his soldiers to either tear down or burn all of the buildings in the town. He strengthened his defenses by mounting all of the fort's sixteen artillery pieces atop the five bastions, and ordered that barrels of water be strategically placed around the compound in case the enemy launched fire arrows into the fort. On May 30, Ecuyer hurried off a dispatch to Colonel Bouquet in Philadelphia stating, "I think the uprising is general; I tremble for our posts. I think according to reports that I am surrounded by Indians. I am neglecting nothing to give them a good reception, and I believe we shall be attacked tomorrow morning."

Instead of launching an all-out assault against the fort, the Indians kept Ecuyer and his men hemmed in while sending war parties to attack the smaller outposts to the north and east. On June 16, the Indians set fire to Fort Venango, killing the entire fifteen-man garrison.

Two days later, Fort Le Boeuf fell to the enemy, but the garrison had managed to escape during the night, the men eventually making their way to the safety of Fort Pitt. On June 20, a war party of Senecas and Delawares were joined by Pontiac's Ottawas, Chippewas, and Hurons in an assault against Fort Presque Isle. After two days of fighting, the thirty-man garrison surrendered to the Indians. After dividing up their captives, the warriors returned to Detroit and Pittsburgh.

To the east, Indian warriors made several attacks against Fort Ligonier and launched raids upon the unsuspecting settlers living on the frontier. Thousands of refugees fled their homes to seek sanctuary in more established communities at Shippensburg, Carlisle, and Lancaster. In the span of just six weeks, the tribes of the Ohio Country and Great Lakes had managed to wipe out nine British outposts, sever the lines of communication from New York and Philadelphia, destroy hundreds of frontier homesteads, and lay siege to both Fort Pitt and Fort Detroit.

From his headquarters in New York City, General Amherst was at first skeptical regarding the alarming news he received from the west. In a letter to Colonel Bouquet he dismissed the reports by writing, "I am persuaded this Alarm will End in Nothing . . . The Post of Fort Pitt, or any of the Others Commanded by Officers, can certainly never be in Danger from such a Wretched Enemy as the Indians." Within days Amherst was forced to admit, "I find the Affair of the Indians, appears to be more General than I had Apprehended." He quickly dispatched to Bouquet the only troops at his disposal—the remnants of two Highland battalions. These Scots had recently returned from campaigning in the Caribbean, and many were still recuperating from the effects of yellow fever.

It took Bouquet more than a month to organize and supply his relief expedition. His command included the two Highland detachments from the 42nd and 77th Regiments of Foot and several companies of the Royal American Regiment, in all less than five hundred men. On July 15, the expedition departed Carlisle and headed westward to clear the line of communication and bring relief to Fort Pitt. Throughout the summer, the redcoats at the fort had been fighting a desperate battle against a combined force of Mingoes, Delawares, Shawnees, Ottawas, and Hurons. Food supplies began to run low, and to make matters worse, smallpox had broken out at the fort. To prevent the spread of the disease, Ecuyer placed the victims in quarantine under the fort's drawbridge. When a delegation of Indian chiefs came to demand that the garrison surrender, the captain attempted to infect them by giving them blankets from the smallpox hospital.

On July 26, another group of chiefs came to the gates of the fort to give Ecuyer one last chance to surrender. The captain defiantly refused, saying "I will not abandon this Post; I have Warriors, Provisions, and Ammunition plenty to defend it three Years against all the Indians in the Woods, and we shall not abandon it as long as a white Man Lives in America."

The day after the parley, the British inside Fort Pitt observed Indians crossing over the river to take up position close to the ramparts. Protected by the riverbanks the warriors unleashed a hot fire against the redcoats that lasted all day and night. During the attack, one soldier was killed and seven wounded, including Ecuyer, whose left leg was grazed by an arrow. The Indians approached so close that they were able to launch fire arrows into the fort and damaged the commandant's house and

KIASUTHA

One of the most important Indian leaders to emerge during Fort Pitt's long and colorful history was the Seneca chief Kiasutha, also spelled Guyasuta. Born among the Genesee River Senecas, his name meant "it sets up the cross" or "crosses standing in a row," perhaps due to an early association with European missionaries. Initially he seemed well disposed toward the British, and as a young man he served as a guide to George Washington on his diplomatic mission to demand French evacuation of the Ohio Country in 1753. Later, however, he gravitated to the French sphere of influence and was perhaps one of the few Iroquois who participated in Braddock's defeat at the Monongahela. From that time on, Kiasutha demonstrated his implacable resentment toward the British.

In the summer of 1761, Kiasutha and another Seneca warrior named Tahaiadoris carried a red war belt to the Indians living near Fort Detroit. They claimed that they were emissaries from the Ohio Country tribes and had come to encourage the Great Lakes warriors to join them in a war against the British. In a council, Kiasutha urged the assembled Indians to "strike immediately" before the redcoats had an opportunity to "fortify themselves." Kiasutha's plot was uncovered when an Indian friendly to the British warned Fort Detroit's commander. Having lost the element of surprise, the two Seneca envoys returned to the upper Ohio River Valley. Years later, historians credited Pontiac with formulating the plan to wipe out the British on the frontier. In fact, the basic elements of the plot were developed by Kiasutha two years before the uprising took place.

During the Indian uprising of 1763, Kiasutha was a principal leader in the siege of Fort Pitt and perhaps orchestrated the attacks against Venango, Le Boeuf, and Presque Isle. There is debate among historians regarding his presence at the Battle of Bushy Run. Simon Girty, the renegade who fought alongside the Indians during the American Revolution, once claimed in a deposition that he had heard Kiasutha say he was in the engagement, and that he was in command during the attack on Colonel Bouquet.

When Bouquet led his expedition against the Ohio Country tribes in 1764, Kiasutha must have realized that further resistance was futile. He served as the principal spokesman for the Indians during negotiations with Bouquet. Afterward, he worked closely with the Indian super-

the barracks. Undaunted, the women of the garrison formed a bucket brigade and quenched the flames.

The Indians continued their attack on Fort Pitt until the afternoon of August 1, when they all departed to ambush Colonel Bouquet's approaching army. The woodland warriors met the relief force near Bushy Run, about twenty-five miles east of Pittsburgh. For two days, the combined native force kept Bouquet's men pinned down, inflicting more than one hundred casualties. Just when it seemed that the British position was about to be overrun, Bouquet launched a brilliant counterattack that succeeded in killing many of the Indians and sending the rest fleeing through the forest. After the Battle of Bushy Run, the tribes abandoned their siege against Fort Pitt and retreated deep into their sanctuaries along the Muskingum and Cuyahoga Rivers. Bouquet's victorious but battered command reached the fort on August 10, much to the consolation of Ecuyer and his beleaguered garrison.

With the relief of Fort Pitt and Pontiac's inability to take Fort Detroit, the Indian uprising subsided during the fall of 1763. The following year, Bouquet assembled an offensive force of twelve hundred men at Fort Pitt for a punitive expedition deep into Indian territory. When his command neared their villages intendent, Sir William Johnson, to preserve the uneasy peace that had been made with the British. Due largely to his efforts, the Senecas and Delawares refused to join the Shawnee during Lord Dunmore's War.

During the Revolution, Kiasutha tried to keep his Ohio Country Indians neutral. Nonetheless, at a conference at Fort Pitt in 1776, he told the Americans, "I am appointed by the Six Nations [the Iroquois Confederation] to take care of this country, that is of the nations on the other side of the Ohio, and I desire you will not think of an expedition against Detroit, for, I repeat, we will not suffer an army to pass through our country." When the Indians finally broke their neutrality, Kiasutha reluctantly "took up the hatchet" against the Americans. Most historians agree that he was the leader of the Indian attack against Hannastown in 1782.

After the war, Kiasutha sold his property near present-day Sharpsburg to James O'Hara. According to one source, O'Hara "gave the old chief a home on [his] plantation during his declining years. Here he died some time in the closing years of the eighteenth century, and his body was placed in the old Indian mound on the estate." Another account claims that Kiasutha died at the old Delaware village known as Custaloga's Town, located along

Kiasutha. *The Seneca chief helped plan the Indian war against the British and partici-pated in the 1763 siege on Fort Pitt. He later fought against the Americans in the Revolution.* LAWRENCE COUNTY HISTORICAL SOCIETY, NEWCASTLE, PA

French Creek in present-day Mercer County. A third version maintains that the chief died on the Cornplanter Indian grant in present-day Warren County.

along the Muskingum, tribal leaders came forward to discuss peace terms. Bouquet demanded that the Indians give up all the captives they had in their possession and send delegates to negotiate a final peace treaty with Sir William Johnson, superintendent of Indian Affairs. The Seneca chief Kiasutha, who had been an important leader during the siege against Fort Pitt, assured Bouquet, "Now we have thrown everything bad away & nothing remains in our Heart but Good."

With the Indian uprising at an end, the settlers returned to their homes and began to rebuild. While the community of Pittsburgh once again began to grow, the fort itself suffered from neglect. No

longer fearing Indian attacks, Bouquet recommended that the fort be converted into a trading post. In April 1765, the Royal engineer Harry Gordon ordered that no further works be constructed at the fort. A survey of the compound made for Gen. Thomas Gage in 1766 noted that the barracks, chimneys, and underground powder magazines had badly deteriorated.

By 1772, the British government saw no further need in maintaining troops on the frontier. Revolutionary agitation in the eastern seaboard communities mandated that the handful of redcoats at Fort Pitt be withdrawn to serve as a constabulary in Philadelphia. When the

John Murray, Fourth Earl of Dunmore.
In 1774 the Virginia governor sent an envoy
to Fort Pitt to lay claim to the region for the
colony. His efforts to shore up Virginia's hold
on the area sparked conflict with the Indians.

same man who had built Trent's Fort two decades earlier. Presumably, Ward used it as a trading post.

In January 1774, Virginia governor John Murray, the fourth earl of Dunmore, decided to reassert his colony's jurisdictional claim to the Forks of the Ohio, an issue that had remained unresolved during the French and Indian War. Lord Dunmore sent Dr. John Connolly to Pittsburgh to eject Ward from the fort and assume control over the region. Connolly claimed authority to organize a new county government and called for loyal settlers to organize a militia to defend Virginia's claims. This militia took over Fort Pitt and renamed the outpost Fort Dunmore in honor of the governor. Pennsylvania authorities seemed powerless to stop expansionist plans, since most of the frontiersmen living in the Ohio Country were loyal to Virginia.

To strengthen Virginia's claims to the Ohio Country, Dunmore and Connolly encouraged settlers and speculators to stake claims to the region, a move that violated promises with the Indians living in the vicinity. Such close contact between land-hungry whites and Indians ensured conflict. In April 1774, Virginians attacked a Shawnee trading party along the Ohio River near present-day Wheeling, West Virginia. Several days later, another group of Virginians murdered ten peaceful Mingo Indians settled along the mouth of Yellow Creek, near present-day Wellsville, Ohio. In retaliation for this attack against his kinsmen, the Mingo chief Logan launched raids against unwary settlers on the frontier. Dunmore wasted no time in declaring war against the Indians, primarily as an excuse to force land concessions from them. The governor raised a militia force of nearly three thousand men that struck Shawnee and Mingo villages deep in the

missionary David McClure visited the fort in October, he recorded in his journal: "In consequence of orders from General Gage, the garrison are preparing to depart. They have begun to destroy the fortress." McClure noted that many of the local inhabitants were distressed over the move, fearing the consequences in the event of another Indian war. When McClure inquired about the abandonment of the post, a British officer replied, "the Americans will not submit to the British Parliament and they may now defend themselves."

On October 10, the fort's commander, Maj. Charles Edmonstone, sold all the building materials in the outpost, including the bricks, stone, iron, and timber, to William Thompson and Alexander Ross. Rather than demolish the fort, Thompson and Ross leased the compound to Maj. Edward Ward, the

Ohio Country. In the fall of 1774, Dunmore's War came to an end when the militia decisively defeated the Indians at the Battle of Point Pleasant and forced them to cede all their land south of the Ohio River.

Lord Dunmore's reign in Virginia came to an abrupt end in 1775, when a patriot uprising against British rule forced the loyalist governor to flee for his life. His hasty departure did not resolve the boundary dispute between Pennsylvania and Virginia, however. With the outbreak of the American Revolution, the newly formed Continental Congress pleaded with Pennsylvania and Virginia to set aside their differences and accept an armistice. As a result, a final boundary was not run until 1786.

THE AMERICAN REVOLUTION ON THE FRONTIER

Revolutionary sentiment was not confined to the Atlantic seaboard communities of Boston and Philadelphia. Settlers at Pittsburgh were also fed up with British policies, especially as they related to land issues and Indian affairs. Like Boston, Pittsburgh had its own tea party in August 1775, when a group of patriots burst into a store and confronted the owners, Joseph Symonds and John Campbell, who were selling tea "in open contempt and defiance of the Resolves of the Continental Congress." The angry crowd confiscated the tea and destroyed it at the foot of a Liberty pole. The spirit of independence was also apparent at nearby Hannastown, where the Westmoreland County Committee adopted resolutions remarkably similar in context to language used in the Declaration of Independence, a full year before that document was adopted by the Second Continental Congress.

As Great Britain and the Colonies moved closer to war, backcountry patriots became increasingly concerned over a possible alliance between the British and the various Indian tribes that inhabited the Ohio Country. To gain assurances of Indian neutrality in the event of war, American commissioners from Virginia met with Iroquois, Delaware, and Shawnee leaders at Fort Pitt in the fall of 1775, and promised to respect their sovereignty over Indian land.

American efforts to maintain peace with the Indians did not deter the British from attempting to win the loyalty of the various tribes. In October 1776, British military officials ordered Gen. Henry Hamilton to enlist the support of the Indian nations in the war against the Americans. To induce the Indians to wreak havoc on the frontier, Hamilton offered bounties for the settlers' scalps. The Americans soon referred to the general as the "hair buyer." Within months, Hamilton was pleased to report to his superiors that his Indian allies had killed or captured 115 people.

As Indian raids on the frontier escalated, settlers found themselves running desperately low on gunpowder. It was difficult to obtain powder from the east, and transporting the precious commodity over the mountains was risky since it might fall into the hands of the enemy.

Edward Hand. Within three years of arriving from Ireland in 1774, Dr. Hand was a Continental Army general, in command of the Western District. His tenure was plagued by setbacks, and he asked to be relieved after eleven months. INDEPENDENCE NATIONAL HISTORICAL PARK

Lachlan McIntosh. The Scottish-born general from Georgia replaced Edward Hand in the spring of 1778. Like his predecessor, he faced a series of difficulties and also requested relief within eleven months.
INDEPENDENCE NATIONAL HISTORICAL PARK

Finally, two intrepid militia officers, Capt. George Gibson and Lt. William Linn, proposed mounting an expedition to Louisiana in an attempt to purchase a supply of powder from the Spanish. Departing Fort Pitt in July 1776, Gibson, Linn, and fifteen intrepid volunteers descended the Ohio and Mississippi Rivers to New Orleans. Using letters of credit from a Philadelphia merchant, the men were able to secure twelve thousand pounds of gunpowder. While Gibson escorted a portion of the cargo to Philadelphia via a sailing vessel, Linn and the rest of the men loaded the remainder of the powder onto the flatboats and polled their way back home, arriving safely in Pittsburgh in May 1777.

On June 1, 1777, Gen. Edward Hand of the Continental Army arrived at Fort Pitt to assume command over the Western District. Hand was anxious to organize an expedition deep into the Ohio Country to destroy a British storehouse that had been established along Lake Erie at the mouth of the Cuyahoga River to provide arms and ammunition to the Indians. With few regular forces at his disposal, the general called out the militia, and the expedition struck out from Fort Pitt on February 15, 1778. Marching up the Beaver River, the command reached the mouth of the Mahoning River, which was too turbulent to cross. With provisions beginning to run low, the general determined to abort his mission and return to Fort Pitt. Then

a member of the expedition discovered fresh Indian tracks. The trail led to a small Delaware town, which General Hand quickly surrounded and attacked. The village contained only an elderly man and several women and children. The rough and ill-disciplined militiamen killed the man and one of the Indian women. Later the expedition encountered another small Delaware village. Here the frustrated and enraged militia killed another three women and a boy. When the column finally returned to Pittsburgh, the more experienced frontiersmen derisively labeled Hand's operation as the "Squaw Campaign."

Not only was General Hand frustrated by his inability to deal decisively with the British and their Indian allies, but he also had to contend with the vexing issue of loyalist sentiment that existed in and around Fort Pitt. Shortly after returning from the Squaw Campaign, three of Hand's most valuable Indian interpreters, Alexander McKee, Matthew Elliott, and Simon Girty, defected to the British. Thereafter, these so-called renegades fought alongside the Indians in their battles against the Americans who defended the frontier during the Revolution. The general also discovered Tory sympathizers among his own garrison. In April 1778, a handful of soldiers, led by Sgt. Alexander Ballentine, planned to blow up Fort Pitt. Fortunately, the plot was thwarted, but Ballentine and his followers managed to escape by stealing a boat and fleeing down the Ohio. A detachment of troops sent out from the fort overtook the deserters and captured the ringleaders, who were eventually executed.

In May 1778, a dejected General Hand asked to be relieved from duty in the Western District. He was replaced by Brig. Gen. Lachlan McIntosh who arrived in Pittsburgh to command two Continental regiments that had been organized in western Pennsylvania: the 8th Pennsylvania, led by Col. Daniel Brodhead, and the 13th Virginia, under Col. William Crawford. Like his predecessor, McIntosh was eager to launch a punitive strike against the enemy. His target was Fort Detroit, an important staging area for the Indian war parties that devastated the frontier. Like General Forbes twenty years earlier, McIntosh decided to march toward his objective with a "protected advance," building forts along the way. He began by dispatching thirteen hundred men down the Ohio to the mouth of the Beaver River to build an outpost named in his honor, Fort McIntosh (present-day Beaver). From here, the army advanced westward into the heart of Delaware Territory along the Tuscarawas River, where they built Fort Laurens (present-day Bolivar, Ohio). General McIntosh assembled the local Indian leaders and demanded that they submit within two weeks. The Indians, taking note of the fact that the Americans were weak and poorly equipped, burst into laughter. When supplies continued to dwindle, McIntosh had no choice but to cease offensive operations. Leaving behind a small garrison at Fort Laurens, the general returned with his main force to Fort McIntosh for the winter. The soldiers left behind at Laurens spent the winter months under almost constant siege and with few supplies. The fort was eventually abandoned in the summer of 1779.

Dejected by failure and broken by harsh frontier service, McIntosh requested to be relieved from command in April 1779. General Washington appointed Col. Daniel Brodhead to assume command at Fort Pitt. By this time, the Indian raids had intensified all along the frontier. Seneca and Mohawk warriors swept through the Cherry Valley in New York and the Wyoming Valley in Pennsylvania, killing and capturing hundreds of settlers. These attacks finally led Washington to plan a punitive expedition against the Iroquois in New York. In June 1779, Gen. John Sullivan struck out from Easton, Pennsylvania, at the head of three thousand troops to destroy the Iroquois towns. At the same time, Colonel Brodhead was ordered to ascend the Allegheny River and attack the Seneca villages. Both of these expeditions succeeded in burning hundreds of Indian homes and destroying their fields, orchards and livestock. Brodhead's forces alone torched more than 130 Seneca houses and carried away $30,000 worth of plunder. While these campaigns had a disastrous effect on the New York Iroquois, the tribes to the west continued their raiding activities in the Ohio River Valley, prompting the Revolutionary government of Pennsylvania to reinstate its scalp bounty in 1780.

Despite the constant threat of Indian attack, the town of Pittsburgh continued to grow during the years of the Revolution and threatened to engulf what was left of Fort Pitt. Brodhead wrote to a member of the Continental Congress, complaining, "The inhabitants of this place are continually encroaching on what I conceive to be the rights of the garrison. They have now the assurance to erect their fences within a few yards of the bastion." The colonel went on to state that, "the blockhouses likewise which are part of the strength of the place are occupied and claimed by private persons to the injury of the service."

Brodhead was also plagued by a chronic lack of supplies for his soldiers. In July 1780, he wrote to General Wash-

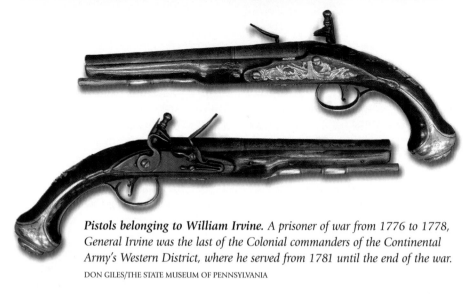

Pistols belonging to William Irvine. A prisoner of war from 1776 to 1778, General Irvine was the last of the Colonial commanders of the Continental Army's Western District, where he served from 1781 until the end of the war.

DON GILES/THE STATE MUSEUM OF PENNSYLVANIA

ington insisting that "there does not remain in our magazines provisions to subsist the troops more than eight days at full rations, nor can I conceive how supplies can be procured in time to prevent their experiencing great want." By the end of January 1781, Brodhead seems to have reached the end of his rope, despairing, "The whole of my present force very little exceeds 300 men, and many of these are unfit for such active service as is necessary here."

In the fall of 1781, Washington removed Brodhead from command and

sent Gen. William Irvine to oversee the garrison at Fort Pitt. Irvine's arrival did nothing to alleviate conditions around Pittsburgh. The citizens agonized over the lack of attention given to their exposed position on the frontier and sent a petition to the Continental Congress asking for further military aid. The appeal began by stating, "We who have the honor of addressing you are a

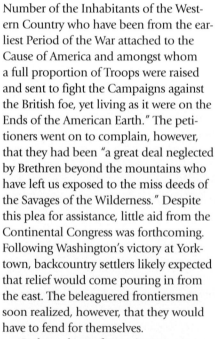

Number of the Inhabitants of the Western Country who have been from the earliest Period of the War attached to the Cause of America and amongst whom a full proportion of Troops were raised and sent to fight the Campaigns against the British foe, yet living as it were on the Ends of the American Earth." The petitioners went on to complain, however, that they had been "a great deal neglected by Brethren beyond the mountains who have left us exposed to the miss deeds of the Savages of the Wilderness." Despite this plea for assistance, little aid from the Continental Congress was forthcoming. Following Washington's victory at Yorktown, backcountry settlers likely expected that relief would come pouring in from the east. The beleaguered frontiersmen soon realized, however, that they would have to fend for themselves.

Perhaps due to frustration over not being able to deal with the elusive warriors who continued to prey upon their settlements, the westerners decided to strike out against a stationary target: the Delaware mission towns along the Tuscarawas River. These Indian villages—Gnadenhutten, Schoenbrun, and Salem—had been founded by the Moravian Church to bring Christianity to the

Indians. As such, the Delawares who lived in these communities took no part in the Indian raids that devastated the frontier. This did not prevent a group of 160 enraged Pennsylvania settlers from swooping down on Gnadenhutten in March 1782. The Delawares living in the town offered no resistance and were quickly captured by the militia. The following day, the Indian men were led two by two to the cooper shop where they were bludgeoned to death with mallets. The settlers took the women and children into the church and brutally executed them as well. In all, the Gnadenhutten Massacre claimed the lives of ninety-four Indian men, women, and children. Before returning to their homes in Washington County, the militia burned all three of the mission towns along the river.

The senseless attack against the peaceful Indians at Gnadenhutten only served to further infuriate the warriors of the Ohio Country. In June 1782, the Indians attacked a militia column near the Sandusky River. The Delawares cap-tured the expedition commander, Col. William Crawford, and burned him at the stake in retaliation for the massacre of their Moravian kinsmen. The following month, a war party of Senecas led by Kiasutha attacked and burned the settle-ment of Hannastown (near present-day Greensburg). While the communities along the eastern seaboard celebrated the Treaty of Paris ending the American Revolution, the frontier continued to be the scene of bloodshed and devastation.

For the next eleven years, sporadic Indian raids against the settlers of west-ern Pennsylvania were commonplace. This resistance to white settlement threat-ened the very existence of the United States government, which needed rev-enue from the sale of public land in the newly created Northwest Territory. When George Washington became president in 1789, he determined to sweep aside the Indian obstacle by force. Once again, Fort Pitt played a role in military affairs, serving as the home for 1st U.S. Infantry and 1st U.S. Artillery and as a storehouse

First Sketch of Pittsburgh. In 1794 Philadelphia merchant Louis Brantz sketched the town that was growing at the forks of the Ohio River. He wrote that "the view from this spot is in truth the most beautiful I ever beheld." CARNEGIE LIBRARY OF PITTSBURGH

for arms and supplies destined to equip the ill-fated military campaigns of Col. Josiah Harmar and Gen. Arthur St. Clair. Both of these officers suffered crushing defeats at the hands of the confederated Indian tribes. It was not until Gen. Anthony Wayne's victory over the Indians at the Battle of Fallen Timbers that peace finally came to the backcountry.

THE FINAL DAYS OF FORT PITT

By the time the American Revolution came to an end, Pittsburgh had grown to such an extent that it seemed unnecessary for Fort Pitt to continue protecting the community. By an agreement made with the Commonwealth of Pennsylvania, the Penn family retained ownership of the forks of the Ohio, and they in turn sold all the property at the tip of the triangle to Isaac Craig and Stephen Bayard, former officers in the Continental Army. The sale touched off a wave of legal disputes from a host of other claimants who maintained that all or part of the property belonged to them. In addition, due to the continuing conflict with the Indians, a small garrison remained at the fort, and the commanding officer refused to allow Craig and Bayard to occupy any

The Blockhouse. This 1908 photograph shows the only remaining structure of Fort Pitt. Col. Henry Bouquet had the redoubt constructed in 1764. PENNSYLVANIA HISTORICAL AND MUSEUM COMMISSION

of the buildings. The two men eventually sold their interest in the fort to a group of partners organized under the name of Turnbull, Marmie and Company. Not waiting for the military to abandon the post, this firm began to dismantle the fort and sell off the building materials. The situation became less problematic in 1792, when the U.S. Army finally withdrew all of its troops from the compound in order to garrison a new post, Fort Fayette, located along the Allegheny River about a quarter mile from Fort Pitt.

After its abandonment by the military, the fort was gradually torn down to make way for new enterprises. Near the turn of the century, Col. James O'Hara, a veteran of the Revolution, built a brewery on the site. According to one observer, "a part of the brew-house premises fills the place which was a bastion." One visitor described the outpost in 1800: "The ramparts of Fort Pitt were still standing, and a portion of the officers' quarters, a substantial brick building, was used as a malt house. The gates were gone, and the brick wall called the revetment, which supported two of the ramparts facing toward the town, and against which officers and soldiers used to play ball, were gone, so that the earth all around had assumed the natural slope." Within a few more years, all that remained of the fort that once guarded the "Gateway to the West" was the blockhouse built in 1764. Industry and commerce, which became the hallmark of Pittsburgh, had finally swallowed up the historic citadel.

POINT STATE PARK AND THE FORT PITT MUSEUM

Throughout the nineteenth and early twentieth centuries Pittsburgh grew to become a thriving metropolis fueled by steel mills. The "Steel City" also gained a reputation as one of America's dirtiest cities, with local blast furnaces and

Pittsburgh in the 1940s. Previously regarded as one of the country's dirtiest cities, Pittsburgh experienced a rejuvenation during the 1940s. State and local officials cleaned the city and developed a park at the confluence of the rivers. PENNSYLVANIA STATE ARCHIVES

smokestacks belching out huge black clouds that caused the streetlights to come on at noon. The property at the famous confluence was regarded as a "blighted area," filled with a host of "nondescript buildings and a sprawling freight terminal." Then in 1943, Pittsburgh's mayor, David L. Lawrence, authorized the formation of the Allegheny Conference on Community Development, a civic organization charged with revitalizing the dingy city. The Allegheny Conference helped arrange capital to clean years of soot from city buildings, build parks, bulldoze slums, and construct cultural and entertainment centers. A ninety-five-acre area near the confluence was cleared to make way for office buildings and hotels.

In 1945, Pennsylvania governor Edward Martin established the Point Park Committee to oversee the construction of a state park at the historic confluence. Charles M. Stotz, one of the leading historic architects in Pennsylvania, and Ralph E. Griswold were selected to design and plan the park. From the beginning these architects decided to maintain a simple composition, where the surrounding hills and rivers would provide "a majestic memorial far more impressive than any manmade monument." In the end, Point State Park reclaimed from the bustling urban landscape a sense of the wilderness environment that existed when Pittsburgh was located at the "Ends of the American Earth."

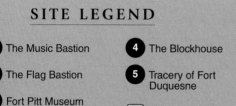

Ohio River

Carson Dr.

Duquesne Incline

837

1 **THE MUSIC BASTION**

Visitors enter Point State Park facing what was once part of the Music Bastion of Fort Pitt. While only a tracery of this bastion remains, a full-scale restoration of a wall section can be seen to the right of the entrance into the museum complex. These walls were originally 15 feet high, 7½ feet thick at the base, and 5 feet thick at the top. Only the eastern face of the fort was reinforced with brick masonry. The other three sides of this pentagonal compound were composed of earth and then covered with blocks of sod usually held in place by wooden pickets. These sod walls were always susceptible to heavy rain and floods. Consequently, it was strictly forbidden to allow animals to graze along the slope lest they would consume all the grass that held the earth in place. After the disastrous flood of 1762, Col. William Eyre reported that the damage done to the bastion facing the Allegheny River was the result of the soldiers' failure to stake down the sod blocks.

2 **THE FLAG BASTION**

At the southeast corner of Point State Park stands the re-created Flag Bastion, a defensive work where the garrison flag was located. Visitors can ascend to the top of this structure, walk along the ramparts, and study the gun embrasures where the fort's cannons were mounted. The vantage point also provides a view of the Monongahela River similar to that seen by eighteenth-century soldiers at Fort Pitt.

Visiting the Site

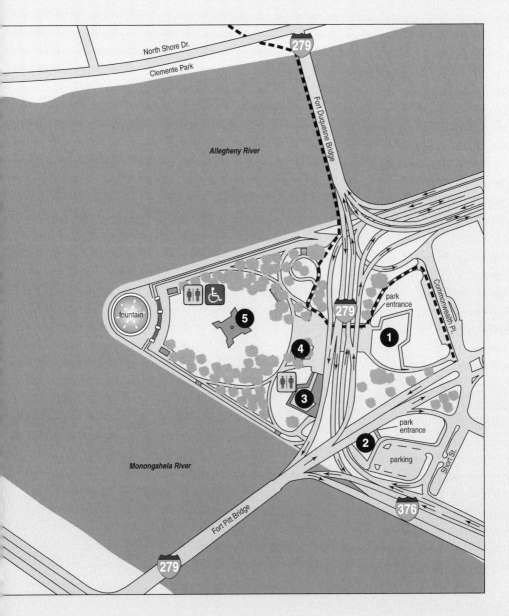

3 FORT PITT MUSEUM

Fort Pitt Museum is housed in the re-created Monongahela Bastion of the fort. Standing in front of the entrance, visitors can examine the cutaway shape of the defensive structure. Upon entering, guests pass through a vestibule where the museum shop is located, and then move to the William Pitt Memorial Hall. Mosaic floor panels designed by sculptor Harry Jackson portray soldier, trader, Indian, missionary, riverman, and settler. William Pitt's coat of arms also is executed in a glass mosaic inlay. The highlight of the hall is a scale model of Fort Pitt based upon original plans preserved in Great Britain's Public Records Office. The model, scaled at one inch to every ten feet, serves as an excellent orientation point. In viewing this replica, it is important to note that the original triangular confluence was much narrower than it is today. The shorelines of both the Monongahela and Allegheny Rivers have been expanded by as much as 250 feet. This means that the actual Point is approximately 430 feet farther downstream than it was in 1758.

Continuing on, visitors enter the exhibit area, which tells the story of the Forks of the Ohio from prehistoric times to the early days of industrialization in Pittsburgh. The exhibits include full rooms, such as a

DON GILES/THE STATE MUSEUM OF PENNSYLVANIA

trader's cabin, soldiers' barracks, and an artillery casemate; interpretive displays featuring authentic period artifacts, paintings, drawings, and maps; small-scale dioramas that portray important events in Fort Pitt's history; and computer-enhanced technology, film presentations, and spoken narratives. Some of the exhibits are part of the museum's permanent collection, and others are shared with other regional historical sites devoted to the French and Indian War era. The museum offers opportunities for group tours and educational programs.

THE BLOCKHOUSE

The only original structure remaining of Fort Pitt today is the Blockhouse, a redoubt constructed under the direction of Col. Henry Bouquet in 1764. The floods that hit Fort Pitt in 1762 and 1763 caused the sod-covered ramparts along the western side of the compound to collapse. Colonel Bouquet wrote to his new commanding officer, Gen. Thomas Gage, "Three sides of this Fort which are not reveted having been rendered almost defenseless by Two successive Floods in 1762, and 1763, I have caused Three Redoubts to be built on the glacis, to cover them. Two are compleated, and the Third going on, as fast as the Weather will permit." One of these redoubts mentioned in Bouquet's letter is the Blockhouse, the oldest authenticated structure in western Pennsylvania.

Perhaps Colonel Bouquet himself designed the redoubt, since his name and the year 1764 are engraved in a stone that is placed above the arched doorway. In February 1764, Capt. William Grant reported to the colonel that he finished the third redoubt and had started construction on "the one you traced out upon the banks of the Monongahela." This would indicate that Bouquet had some hand in the design of these structures. It is also possible that the military cartographer Thomas Hutchins had a hand in the design, since Bouquet appointed him to serve as the fort's engineer throughout the winter of 1763.

During its long history, the redoubt served many purposes other than that for which it was constructed. In 1772, the Indian agent Alexander McKee used the structure as a council house

for meetings with tribal dignitaries. During the famous Whiskey Rebellion, the Blockhouse served as a registration site for the many stills that operated in the region. One long-time resident of Pittsburgh recalled that the Blockhouse once served as an illegal drinking establishment.

After the U.S. Army abandoned the fort in 1792, the old redoubt was occupied for a brief time by William Turnbull. Sometime earlier, Turnbull and his business partners, John Holker and Peter Marmie, had taken bricks from the fort's eastern bastions to build a large addition to the Blockhouse. In 1795, the structure served as the home of Maj. Isaac Craig. His son, Neville, who became one of Pittsburgh's early historians, was born in the redoubt. Shortly afterward, Col. James O'Hara purchased the property and established a brewery on the premises. Presumably, O'Hara rented out the Blockhouse to tenants. W. G. Lyford visited the site in 1837 and reported that the building was occupied by a German family. Lyford suggested to the tenants that they open up the structure for tours. An Englishman named William Ferguson saw the redoubt in 1856 and described it as "a small brick house with arched windows and doorways, now inhabited by the lowest class." Charles Dahlinger, writing in 1922, remembered visiting the historic fortification as a boy. At that time, an Irish family, cognizant of the building's significance, welcomed tourists and sold them candy, lemonade, and cigars.

Over the years the historic building became engulfed by warehouses and railroad terminals. Miraculously, the structure was saved from urban development when Mrs. Mary Elizabeth Schenley, who had inherited the property from her grandfather, Colonel O'Hara, presented the redoubt to the Daughters of the American Revolution (DAR) in 1894. Since then, the DAR has faithfully maintained administration of this remarkable relic. They removed the addition and restored the Blockhouse to its original appearance, even going so far as to retrieve the stone tablet inscribed with Colonel Bouquet's name, which had been removed and placed in the City Hall.

5 TRACERY OF FORT DUQUESNE

Approaching the fountain that graces the Point of the confluence, visitors encounter a full-scale outline of Fort Duquesne formed by stones set into the lawn. In the center of this outline, a large, circular bronze marker depicts a plan of the French fort taken from the only known authentic drawing, which resides in the Bibliotheque Nationale in Paris.

For more information on hours, tours, programs, and activities at Fort Pitt Museum, visit **www.fortpittmuseum.com** or call **412-281-9285**.

Further Reading

Alberts, Robert C. *A Charming Field for an Encounter: The Story of George Washington's Fort Necessity*. Washington, D.C.: U.S. Government Printing Office, 1991.

Anderson, Fred. *Crucible of War: The Seven Years' War and the Fate of Empire in British North America, 1754–1766*. Knopf, 2000.

Brumwell, Stephen. *Redcoats: The British Soldier and War in the Americas, 1755–1763*. Cambridge, U.K.: Cambridge University Press, 2002.

Dahlinger, Charles W. *Fort Pitt*. Pittsburgh: privately printed, 1922.

Dixon, David. *"Never Come to Peace Again": The Pontiac Indian Uprising, 1763–1765*. Norman: University of Oklahoma Press, 2004.

Hunter, William A. *Forts on the Pennsylvania Frontier*. Lewisburg, Pa.: Wennawoods Publishing, 1999.

James, Alfred Proctor, and Charles M. Stotz. *Drums in the Forest*. Pittsburgh: Historical Society of Western Pennsylvania, 1958.

Kent, Donald H. *The French Invasion of Western Pennsylvania*. Harrisburg: Pennsylvania Historical and Museum Commission, 1954.

Kopperman, Paul E. *Braddock at the Monongahela*. Pittsburgh: University of Pittsburgh Press, 1977.

McConnell, Michael N. *A Country Between: The Upper Ohio River Valley and Its Peoples, 1724–1774*. Lincoln: University of Nebraska Press, 1992.

Montgomery, Thomas Lynch, ed. *Report of the Commission to Locate the Site of the Frontier Forts of Pennsylvania*, 2 vols. Harrisburg, Pa.: W. Stanley Ray, 1916.

O'Mera, Walter. *Guns at the Forks*. Englewood Cliffs, N.J.: Prentice Hall, 1965.

Sipe, C. Hale. *Fort Ligonier and Its Times*. Harrisburg, Pa.: Telegraph Press, 1932.

Stevens, S. K., Donald Kent, Autumn Leonard, and Louis Waddell, eds. *The Papers of Henry Bouquet*. 6 vols. Harrisburg: Pennsylvania Historical and Museum Commission, 1972–1994.

Stotz, Charles Morse. *Point of Empire: Conflict at the Forks of the Ohio*. Pittsburgh: Historical Society of Western Pennsylvania, 1970.

Waddell, Louis M., and Bruce D. Bomberger. *The French and Indian War in Pennsylvania, 1753–1763*. Harrisburg: Pennsylvania Historical and Museum Commission, 1996.

West, Martin J. *War for Empire in Western Pennsylvania*. Ligonier, Pa.: Fort Ligonier Association, 1993.

Also Available

Anthracite Heritage Museum
and Scranton Iron Furnaces

Brandywine Battlefield Park

Bushy Run Battlefield

Conrad Weiser Homestead

Cornwall Iron Furnace

Daniel Boone Homestead

Drake Well Museum and Park

Eckley Miners' Village

Ephrata Cloister

Erie Maritime Museum and
U.S. Brig Niagara

Graeme Park

Hope Lodge and Mather Mill

Joseph Priestley House

Landis Valley Museum

Old Economy Village

Pennsbury Manor

Railroad Museum of Pennsylvania

Somerset Historical Center

Washington Crossing Historic Park

All titles are $10, plus shipping,
from Stackpole Books, 800-732-3669, www.stackpolebooks.com, or
The Pennsylvania Historical and Museum Commission, 800-747-7790,
www.phmc.state.pa.us